6. How does inference help in comprehension?

a) It provides direct meanings

b) It draws conclusions based on hints in the text

c) It skips over difficult parts

d) It reduces reading time

Answer: b

7. What is the purpose of asking inferential questions?

a) To assess memorisation

b) To evaluate analytical thinking

c) To test grammar

d) To assess spelling skills

Answer: b

8. Which is NOT a method to improve comprehension?

a) Skimming

b) Scanning

c) Guessing answers

d) Summarizing

Answer: c

9 .Which reading strategy involves searching for specific details?

a) Predicting

b) Skimming

c) Scanning

d) Visualizing

Answer: c

10 .Which question type challenges deeper understanding?

a) True/False

b) Open-ended

c) Multiple-choice

d) Matching

Answer: b

Preface

Welcome to the CTET Paper 2 Class VI to VIII Language 2 Book!

Teaching is a journey of learning, discovery, and personal growth. This book is designed to support you on that journey as you prepare for the Central Teacher Eligibility Test (CTET). Whether you are an aspiring educator or looking to enhance your knowledge, this book will equip you with essential concepts, strategies, and insights to excel in the exam and in your future teaching career.

Our goal is to make your learning experience meaningful and effective. Each chapter in this book has been carefully crafted to engage both your curiosity and critical thinking, covering core topics essential for the CTET exam. Along the way, you will find opportunities to reflect on best practices in education, the role of teachers in shaping society, and the importance of fostering an inclusive and supportive learning environment.

Table of Contents

Chapter 1: Questions

1. What is the goal of reading comprehension activities?

a) Memorizing the text

b) Understanding the text's meaning

c) Practicing handwriting

d) Counting words

Answer: b

2. Which strategy is effective for a quick understanding of the text?

a) Reading aloud slowly

b) Skimming the content

c) Memorizing sentences

d) Writing summaries

Answer: b

3. What type of question asks for direct information from a text?

a) Inferential

b) Literal

c) Subjective

d) Analytical

Answer: b

4. Which is a key feature of unseen prose passages?

a) They are already studied in class

b) They introduce new content for assessment

c) They are purely fiction-based

d) They always include questions on vocabulary

Answer: b

5. What skill is developed through prediction in reading?

a) Decoding words

b) Drawing conclusions

c) Copying text

d) Listening skills

Answer: b

11. What is the focus of the communicative approach in language teaching?

a) Grammar memorisation

b) Language use in real situations

c) Translation exercises

d) Written tests only

Answer: b

12. What is scaffolding in the context of teaching?

a) A building activity

b) Temporary learning support

c) Final assessment strategy

d) Grammar-focused teaching

Answer: b

13. What is an example of natural language acquisition?

a) Learning to speak at home

b) Memorizing vocabulary

c) Practicing grammar exercises

d) Taking language tests

Answer: a

14. Who is known for the Input Hypothesis in language learning?

a) Noam Chomsky

b) Stephen Krashen

c) B.F. Skinner

d) Jean Piaget

Answer: b

15. What is the primary focus of the behaviourist theory?

a) Understanding meaning

b) Learning through repetition and reinforcement

c) Using language creatively

d) Promoting self-correction

Answer: b

16. What does differentiated instruction address?

a) The same teaching method for all students

b) The varied learning needs of students

c) Avoiding group work

d) Ignoring struggling learners

Answer: b

17. What is the role of peer interaction in language learning?

a) It limits individual work

b) It fosters communication skills

c) It reduces the learning pace

d) It increases grammar practice

Answer: b

18. Which principle emphasises "learning by doing"?

a) Constructivist

b) Behaviorist

c) Traditional lecture method

d) Grammar-translation

Answer: a

19. Which language skill is primarily developed through storytelling?

a) Reading only

b) Listening and speaking

c) Memorization

d) Grammar accuracy

Answer: b

20. What is an essential feature of remedial teaching?

a) Covering the syllabus quickly

b) Addressing individual learning gaps

c) Introducing advanced topics

d) Skipping assessments

Answer: b

21. Which type of assessment evaluates comprehension best?

a) Spelling test

b) Cloze test

c) Multiple-choice questions

d) True/False questions

Answer: b

22. What is the challenge of teaching language in a diverse classroom?

a) Identical language proficiency

b) Varying language skills among students

c) Limited content resources

d) No need for differentiation

Answer: b

23. How can a teacher promote effective listening in class?

a) Giving frequent grammar tests

b) Using engaging audio materials

c) Assigning silent reading tasks

d) Increasing homework

Answer: b

24. What is the primary goal of formative assessment in language teaching?

a) To assign grades

b) To monitor student progress and provide feedback

c) To rank students

d) To prepare students for exams

Answer: b

25. What is an example of an audio-visual teaching aid?

a) Flashcards

b) Videos

c) Textbooks

d) Handouts

Answer: b

26. What is the benefit of role-play in language learning?

a) It limits interaction

b) It develops speaking skills

c) It focuses only on grammar

d) It reduces classroom time

Answer: b

27. What is the aim of remedial teaching?

a) To push students to new topics

b) To reinforce areas where students struggle

c) To increase homework

d) To speed up the syllabus

Answer: b

28. Which language skill does dictation improve?

a) Reading only

b) Listening and writing

c) Speaking only

d) Memorization

Answer: b

29. What is essential for evaluating language proficiency?

a) Spelling tests

b) Listening, speaking, reading, and writing assessments

c) Memorization exercises

d) Handwriting tests

Answer: b

30. How can a teacher manage a diverse classroom?

a) By ignoring differences

b) By using differentiated instruction

c) By giving the same task to all students

d) By limiting group activities

Answer: b

31. What helps improve reading comprehension?

a) Memorizing sentences

b) Making predictions and summaries

c) Ignoring difficult words

d) Writing paragraphs

Answer: b

32. What kind of questions are used in Cloze tests?

a) Yes/No

b) Fillintheblank with missing words

c) Matching columns

d) True/False

Answer: b

33. What role does vocabulary play in reading comprehension?

a) It helps in writing essays

b) It supports understanding of the text

c) It increases reading speed

d) It promotes memorisation

Answer: b

34. Which activity enhances language fluency?

a) Silent reading

b) Group discussions and debates

c) Copying text repeatedly

d) Writing essays only

Answer: b

35. What **is a receptive language skill?**

a) Reading and writing

b) Listening and reading

c) Speaking and writing

d) Speaking and listening

Answer: b

36. Which is a productive language skill?

a) Reading

b) Listening

c) Writing

d) Memorizing

Answer: c

37. What is the primary role of listening in communication?

a) Improving handwriting

b) Understanding messages effectively

c) Replacing speaking

d) Increasing vocabulary only

Answer: b

38. Which activity strengthens both listening and speaking skills?

a) Dictation

b) Group discussions

c) Silent reading

d) Writing stories

Answer: b

39. What is an example of summative assessment?

a) A final exam

b) Weekly quizzes

c) Class discussions

d) Daily homework

Answer: a

40. Which factor contributes most to second language acquisition?

a) Natural exposure to the language

b) Memorizing grammar rules

c) Writing summaries daily

d) Taking exams frequently

Answer: a

41. Which theory emphasises learning through interaction?

a) Behaviorist

b) Social constructivist

c) Grammar-translation

d) Cognitive load theory

Answer: b

42. What is peer teaching?

a) Students teaching each other

b) Teachers teaching groups only

c) Self-learning through books

d) Learning through technology

Answer: a

43. Which method develops reading fluency best?

a) Reading aloud regularly

b) Listening to songs only

c) Watching videos

d) Skipping difficult words

Answer: a

44. What is the aim of formative assessment?

a) Identifying areas for improvement

b) Ranking students

c) Assigning final grades

d) Reducing learning time

Answer: a

45. Which teaching material is most suitable for early readers?

a) Complex novels

b) Picture books

c) Newspapers

d) Research articles

Answer: b

46. Which strategy is least effective in teaching vocabulary?

a) Flashcards

b) Memorizing word lists

c) Contextual learning

d) Games and activities

Answer: b

47. Which approach focuses on student participation?

a) Lecture-based

b) Communicative approach

c) Silent reading method

d) Memorization drills

Answer: b

48. How does cultural diversity affect language learning?

a) It complicates language teaching

b) It enriches the learning environment

c) It reduces interaction

d) It has no impact

Answer: b

49. Which principle guides differentiated instruction?

a) One size fits all

b) Tailoring teaching to student needs

c) Rote learning for everyone

d) Using only textbooks

Answer: b

50. What does phonemic awareness help develop?

a) Reading fluency

b) Listening comprehension

c) Vocabulary

d) Grammar skills

Answer: a

51. Which activity improves spelling skills?

a) Dictation

b) Listening exercises

c) Roleplay

d) Watching videos

Answer: a

52. What is the purpose of remedial teaching?

a) To introduce new topics

b) To help struggling learners

c) To reduce syllabus content

d) To assign more homework

Answer: b

53. Which assessment type provides real-time feedback?

a) Formative

b) Summative

c) Diagnostic

d) Norm-referenced

Answer: a

54. What type of question encourages critical thinking?

a) True/False

b) Multiple-choice

c) Open-ended

d) Matching

Answer: c

55. What is a challenge in large classrooms?

a) Too few resources

b) Managing individual attention

c) Overuse of textbooks

d) Limited syllabus coverage

Answer: b

56. What promotes language fluency in speaking?

a) Silent reading

b) Frequent speaking practice

c) Memorizing conversations

d) Only listening activities

Answer: b

57. Which tool helps assess listening comprehension?

a) Audio recordings with questions

b) Grammar worksheets

c) Reading passages

d) Writing tests

Answer: a

58. Which material supports interactive learning?

a) Flashcards

b) Interactive whiteboards

c) Printed handouts

d) Textbooks

Answer: b

59. What is the role of feedback in learning?

a) To discourage mistakes

b) To guide improvement

c) To assign grades only

d) To reduce participation

Answer: b

60. Which activity encourages collaborative learning?

a) Group projects

b) Silent reading

c) Independent study

d) Memorization

Answer: a

61. What is the purpose of diagnostic assessment?

a) To assign grades

b) To identify learning gaps

c) To rank students

d) To finish the syllabus

Answer: b

62. Which method emphasises learning through repetition?

a) Behaviorist approach

b) Constructivist approach

c) Cognitive theory

d) Social learning theory

Answer: a

63. How does role play benefit students?

a) Reduces participation

b) Develops speaking skills

c) Promotes silent learning

d) Increases memorisation

Answer: b

64. Which skill does reading aloud improve?

a) Listening only

b) Reading fluency

c) Grammar accuracy

d) Handwriting

Answer: b

65. What supports vocabulary development best?

a) Flashcards and games

b) Grammar exercises

c) Writing essays

d) Dictation only

Answer: a

66. Which teaching strategy helps engage all students?

a) Lecture-based teaching

b) Group discussions and activities

c) Memorization

d) Silent reading

Answer: b

67. Which method helps assess reading fluency?

a) Reading aloud with timing

b) Grammar tests

c) Listening exercises

d) Writing summaries

Answer: a

68. Which tool supports individualized learning?

a) Adaptive software

b) Printed textbooks

c) Blackboards

d) Group assessments

Answer: a

69. Which material best supports young learners?

a) Picture books

b) Research papers

c) Academic journals

d) Newspapers

Answer: a

70. Which teaching style promotes creativity?

a) Rote learning

b) Project-based learning

c) Memorization

d) Lecture method

Answer: b

71. Which method improves listening comprehension?

a) Passive listening

b) Active listening with note-taking

c) Reading silently

d) Memorizing speeches

Answer: b

72. What is the most effective way to build reading fluency?

a) Timed repeated readings

b) Listening to audiobooks only

c) Skimming difficult texts

d) Memorizing paragraphs

Answer: a

73. Which factor enhances second language acquisition?

a) Limited exposure to native speakers

b) Constant grammar correction

c) Rich, meaningful language input

d) Memorizing isolated vocabulary

Answer: c

74. What is an example of real-world language use?

a) Filling in worksheets

b) Ordering food at a restaurant

c) Copying text from a book

d) Taking a spelling test

Answer: b

75. What promotes student engagement in language learning?

a) Lengthy lectures

b) Group projects and collaboration

c) Independent textbook reading

d) Rote memorization drills

Answer: b

76. Which type of assessment measures long-term retention?

a) Formative

b) Summative

c) Diagnostic

d) Criterion-referenced

Answer: b

77. Which activity promotes collaborative learning?

a) Independent reading

b) Debate and discussion

c) Grammar drills

d) Silent note-taking

Answer: b

78. Which is a principle of effective language teaching?

a) Focus only on written skills

b) Balance between input and output activities

c) Teach grammar exclusively

d) Avoid peer interaction

Answer: b

79. Which tool helps assess vocabulary knowledge?

a) Cloze tests

b) Oral presentations

c) Essay writing

d) Sentence diagrams

Answer: a

80. How does multimedia enhance language teaching?

a) Reduces class interaction

b) Provides visual and auditory learning support

c) Limits student focus

d) Replaces textbooks entirely

Answer: b

81. What is the focus of task-based learning?

a) Memorizing grammar rules

b) Completing meaningful tasks

c) Reading textbooks only

d) Writing long essays

Answer: b

82. Which activity builds oral fluency?

a) Essay writing

b) Debate competitions

c) Multiple-choice quizzes

d) Dictation

Answer: b

83. What is formative assessment used for?

a) To grade final exams

b) To provide ongoing feedback

c) To eliminate weak students

d) To reduce teaching time

Answer: b

84. How does peer feedback benefit students?

a) It reduces participation

b) It helps identify areas for improvement

c) It discourages collaboration

d) It leads to conflicts

Answer: b

85. What is the aim of interactive reading?

a) Passive consumption of text

b) Active engagement with the material

c) Memorizing paragraphs

d) Writing summaries only

Answer: b

86. Which teaching material encourages active learning?

a) Flashcards

b) Printed handouts

c) Interactive whiteboards

d) Silent reading books

Answer: c

87. What is an example of informal assessment?

a) Midterm exams

b) Class discussions

c) Standardized tests

d) Final projects

Answer: b

88. What helps develop listening comprehension?

a) Grammar worksheets

b) Audiobooks and discussions

c) Silent reading

d) Writing essays

Answer: b

89. Which skill is assessed by oral presentations?

a) Writing

b) Reading comprehension

c) Speaking proficiency

d) Listening

Answer: c

90. Which technique supports diverse learners?

a) Differentiated instruction

b) Lecture-based teaching only

c) Memorization of content

d) One-size-fits-all teaching

Answer: a

91. Which activity develops collaborative skills?

a) Group problem-solving

b) Silent study

c) Independent writing

d) Grammar drills

Answer: a

92. How can teachers manage mixed-ability classrooms?

a) By assigning the same tasks to all

b) By using flexible grouping

c) By focusing only on fast learners

d) By reducing group activities

Answer: b

93. What encourages language practice in class?

a) Restricting speaking time

b) Creating real-life scenarios

c) Limiting communication to written tasks

d) Avoiding peer interaction

Answer: b

94. Which skill is strengthened by storytelling?

a) Vocabulary memorization

b) Listening and speaking

c) Handwriting improvement

d) Grammar practice

Answer: b

95. What supports remedial learners the most?

a) Assigning extra homework

b) Providing targeted interventions

c) Ignoring their difficulties

d) Teaching at a faster pace

Answer: b

96. What is the goal of diagnostic assessment?

a) To assign final grades

b) To identify learning gaps

c) To teach new content

d) To rank students

Answer: b

97. Which skill is developed through debate?

a) Listening comprehension

b) Speaking fluency and critical thinking

c) Grammar memorization

d) Reading speed

Answer: b

98. Which method encourages participation?

a) Lecture-based teaching

b) Interactive discussions

c) Silent reading sessions

d) Memorization drills

Answer: b

99. What helps improve spelling proficiency?

a) Dictation exercises

b) Silent reading

c) Multiple-choice quizzes

d) Listening to audiobooks

Answer: a

100. How does differentiated instruction help?

a) By catering to individual learning needs

b) By reducing teaching time

c) By focusing only on fast learners

d) By assigning the same tasks to all students

Answer: a

Chapter 2: Questions

101 .**Which activity promotes vocabulary retention?**

a) Flashcard games

b) Silent reading

c) Grammar translation

d) Listening to music

Answer: a

102. **What is the primary aim of remedial teaching?**

a) To introduce advanced topics

b) To address individual learning difficulties

c) To replace regular instruction

d) To assign extra homework

Answer: b

103. **Which assessment type is best for identifying prior knowledge?**

a) Formative assessment

b) Diagnostic assessment

c) Summative assessment

d) Criterion-referenced assessment

Answer: b

104. **What is a key element of communicative language teaching?**

a) Grammar drills

b) Focus on real-life language use

c) Memorization of rules

d) Translation exercises

Answer: b

105. **Which activity helps build fluency in a second language?**

a) Role-playing conversations

b) Memorizing dictionary definitions

c) Writing long essays

d) Grammar-focused reading

Answer: a

106. **What is the role of listening comprehension in language learning?**

a) Improving pronunciation

b) Enhancing understanding and response

c) Replacing reading practice

d) Memorizing audio scripts

Answer: b

107. **Which strategy improves reading comprehension?**

a) Predicting outcomes and summarizing texts

b) Memorizing each sentence

c) Ignoring unknown words

d) Skipping challenging sections

Answer: a

108 .**Which method fosters critical thinking?**

a) Asking open-ended questions

b) Rote memorization

c) Matching exercises

d) Multiple-choice tests

Answer: a

109. **How can teachers support struggling learners?**

a) By increasing homework

b) By using individualized support plans

c) By reducing class time

d) By ignoring their difficulties

Answer: b

110. **What is the purpose of task-based learning?**

a) To teach grammar rules

b) To complete meaningful tasks in context

c) To memorize vocabulary lists

d) To translate texts

Answer: b

111 .**Which tool promotes active student engagement?**

a) Interactive whiteboards

b) Printed textbooks

c) Silent reading logs

d) Flashcards only

Answer: a

112 .**Which skill is enhanced through debate?**

a) Memorization of rules

b) Critical thinking and fluency

c) Listening only

d) Writing neatly

Answer: b

113. **Which material helps young learners the most?**

a) Research articles

b) Illustrated storybooks

c) Academic papers

d) Complex novels

Answer: b

114. **What is a benefit of using multimedia in the classroom?**

a) It reduces class participation

b) It supports both auditory and visual learning

c) It limits student focus

d) It eliminates the need for textbooks

Answer: b

115. **Which technique encourages collaborative learning?**

a) Group projects and discussions

b) Silent reading sessions

c) Independent study

d) Memorization drills

Answer: a

116. **How does formative assessment benefit students?**

a) It assigns final grades

b) It provides feedback for improvement

c) It reduces class interaction

d) It replaces summative assessment

Answer: b

117. **What promotes oral fluency in a second language?**

a) Silent reading

b) Regular speaking practice

c) Listening without speaking

d) Writing essays

Answer: b

118 .**What is an effective way to teach listening skills?**

a) Grammar worksheets

b) Audiobooks with follow-up discussions

c) Silent note-taking

d) Writing summaries

Answer: b

119 .**Which method supports diverse learners?**

a) Differentiated instruction

b) One-size-fits-all teaching

c) Reducing group work

d) Memorization only

Answer: a

120. **How does peer feedback improve learning?**

a) It discourages participation

b) It identifies areas for growth

c) It reduces motivation

d) It replaces teacher feedback

Answer: b

121 .**Which strategy builds reading fluency?**

a) Timed repeated readings

b) Listening to music

c) Memorizing poems

d) Skipping hard words

Answer: a

122 .**What is the main focus of communicative activities?**

a) Grammar accuracy

b) Language use in real-life scenarios

c) Memorization of definitions

d) Silent reading practice

Answer: b

123 .**Which material fosters active learning?**

a) Flashcards

b) Printed worksheets

c) Interactive apps and games

d) Textbooks only

Answer: c

124. **How do role-play activities benefit students?**

a) They limit interaction

b) They develop speaking and listening skills

c) They focus on grammar only

d) They reduce participation

Answer: b

125. **What is the benefit of diagnostic assessment?**

a) It measures final achievement

b) It identifies learning gaps early

c) It assigns grades only

d) It ranks students

Answer: b

126. **Which approach promotes student-centered learning?**

a) Teacher lectures

b) Group discussions and collaboration

c) Memorization drills

d) Silent study periods

Answer: b

127. **Which activity builds critical thinking in language learning?**

a) Debates and discussions

b) Grammar translation

c) Copying notes

d) Silent reading

Answer: a

128. **Which skill does storytelling enhance?**

a) Grammar

b) Listening and speaking

c) Silent reading

d) Essay writing

Answer: b

129 .**What helps students retain new vocabulary?**

a) Repeated exposure in different contexts

b) Memorizing word lists

c) Writing dictionary definitions

d) Listening passively

Answer: a

130 .**Which tool measures vocabulary proficiency?**

a) Cloze tests

b) Oral presentations

c) Writing samples

d) Sentence completion exercises

Answer: a

131 .**What type of task improves listening skills?**

a) Audiobook with comprehension questions

b) Writing exercises

c) Multiple-choice grammar tests

d) Silent reading

Answer: a

132 .**What role does formative assessment play?**

a) Assigning final grades

b) Providing ongoing feedback

c) Replacing summative assessment

d) Reducing participation

Answer: b

133. **What is the purpose of remedial teaching?**

a) To introduce advanced topics

b) To address learning challenges

c) To skip assessments

d) To assign more homework

Answer: b

134 .**Which strategy promotes vocabulary development?**

a) Contextual learning and games

b) Memorizing definitions only

c) Silent study

d) Writing essays

Answer: a

135. **What is the benefit of peer interaction in language learning?**

a) It reduces speaking opportunities

b) It encourages collaborative learning

c) It focuses only on writing

d) It discourages group work

Answer: b

136 .**Which activity promotes listening and speaking skills?**

a) Role-play

b) Silent reading

c) Grammar tests

d) Essay writing

Answer: a

137. **What is the focus of task-based learning?**

a) Completing meaningful tasks in context

b) Memorizing grammar rules

c) Reading long texts

d) Copying notes

Answer: a

138. **Which strategy encourages student participation?**

a) Interactive discussions

b) Silent study periods

c) Lecture-based teaching

d) Memorization exercises

Answer: a

139 .**Which tool assesses reading comprehension?**

a) Cloze tests

b) Oral presentations

c) Grammar worksheets

d) Spelling tests

Answer: a

140. **What role does listening play in communication?**

a) It replaces reading

b) It enhances understanding and response

c) It limits speaking opportunities

d) It reduces vocabulary use

Answer: b

141. **How does multimedia support language learning?**

a) It makes lessons boring

b) It provides audio-visual learning aids

c) It limits interaction

d) It replaces teacher feedback

Answer: b

142. **Which assessment measures students' language proficiency?**

a) Listening exercises only

b) Comprehensive oral and written tests

c) Multiple-choice quizzes only

d) Spelling competitions

Answer: b

143. **What is an effective strategy for mixed-ability classrooms?**

a) Ignoring individual differences

b) Using differentiated instruction

c) Teaching at a single pace

d) Avoiding group activities

Answer: b

144. **What promotes student engagement in language classes?**

a) Lecture-based teaching

b) Interactive activities and discussions

c) Memorization exercises only

d) Silent study

Answer: b

145. **Which tool measures oral language proficiency?**

a) Cloze test

b) Oral presentation

c) Grammar worksheet

d) Written exam

Answer: b

146. **How do role plays benefit students?**

a) They improve listening and speaking skills

b) They focus only on grammar rules

c) They discourage interaction

d) They reduce student motivation

Answer: a

147. **What is the purpose of group discussions?**

a) To rank students

b) To develop critical thinking and speaking skills

c) To replace individual learning

d) To memorize content

Answer: b

148. **How does peer teaching benefit learners?**

a) It replaces teacher feedback

b) It encourages collaboration and learning from peers

c) It reduces classroom participation

d) It increases individual tasks

Answer: b

149. **Which type of test assesses reading comprehension effectively?**

a) Oral tests

b) Cloze tests

c) Listening comprehension tests

d) Spelling tests

Answer: b

150. **What is a common challenge in a diverse classroom?**

a) Identical learning needs

b) Varying language proficiency levels

c) Availability of unlimited resources

d) All students excelling equally

Answer: b

151. **Which strategy builds vocabulary effectively?**

a) Repeated exposure in different contexts

b) Silent reading only

c) Memorizing dictionary definitions

d) Grammar translation

Answer: a

152. **Which activity fosters collaborative learning?**

a) Independent study

b) Group projects and problem-solving

c) Grammar exercises only

d) Lecture-based teaching

Answer: b

153. **How can teachers support remedial learners?**

a) Ignoring their difficulties

b) Providing targeted interventions

c) Reducing their participation

d) Assigning extra homework

Answer: b

154. **What is a key feature of summative assessment?**

a) Ongoing feedback

b) Measures overall achievement at the end of instruction

c) Identifies learning gaps

d) Provides real-time feedback

Answer: b

155. **What does formative assessment focus on?**

a) Assigning grades

b) Providing continuous feedback to improve learning

c) Eliminating weaker students

d) Ranking students

Answer: b

156. **What helps improve speaking fluency?**

a) Silent reading

b) Frequent opportunities to speak in class

c) Memorizing speeches

d) Listening passively

Answer: b

157. **Which method improves listening comprehension?**

a) Passive listening

b) Active listening with follow-up questions

c) Memorizing grammar rules

d) Copying lecture notes

Answer: b

158. **How does differentiated instruction benefit students?**

a) By catering to individual learning needs

b) By applying the same method for all students

c) By ignoring learning gaps

d) By focusing only on advanced learners

Answer: a

159. **What promotes language learning in young children?**

a) Complex textbooks

b) Play-based learning with songs and stories

c) Memorization exercises

d) Silent reading

Answer: b

160. **What is a benefit of using flashcards for vocabulary learning?**

a) They promote collaborative writing

b) They provide repetitive exposure to words

c) They reduce reading practice

d) They eliminate the need for tests

Answer: b

161. **Which tool enhances student engagement during lessons?**

a) Interactive apps and games

b) Printed worksheets only

c) Silent study logs

d) Long lectures

Answer: a

162. **Which activity strengthens critical thinking?**

a) Memorizing definitions

b) Participating in debates

c) Silent reading

d) Writing summaries only

Answer: b

163. **How does storytelling enhance language skills?**

a) It improves spelling

b) It develops listening and speaking skills

c) It limits reading practice

d) It discourages participation

Answer: b

164. **What supports second language acquisition?**

a) Memorizing grammar rules

b) Meaningful exposure to language use

c) Writing only

d) Reducing speaking practice

Answer: b

165. **How does peer feedback improve learning?**

a) It discourages student collaboration

b) It identifies areas for growth

c) It reduces motivation

d) It replaces teacher input

Answer: b

166. **Which strategy promotes vocabulary retention?**

a) Context-based learning

b) Grammar-only teaching

c) Memorizing lists without context

d) Avoiding new words

Answer: a

167. **What is the role of real-life tasks in language learning?**

a) To assess grammar only

b) To provide meaningful language use

c) To reduce class participation

d) To teach memorization

Answer: b

168. **What is the primary goal of communicative language teaching?**

a) Grammar accuracy

b) Effective communication in real-life situations

c) Memorizing definitions

d) Translation of texts

Answer: b

169. **Which assessment provides real-time feedback to learners?**

a) Formative assessment

b) Summative assessment

c) Diagnostic assessment

d) Criterion-referenced assessment

Answer: a

170. **What supports learners with different proficiency levels?**

a) Using the same method for all students

b) Differentiated instruction

c) Ignoring individual needs

d) Assigning identical tasks

Answer: b

171. **What encourages active student participation?**

a) Interactive discussions and activities

b) Silent study periods

c) Lecture-based instruction

d) Independent note-taking

Answer: a

172. **What builds fluency in listening and speaking?**

a) Role-play activities

b) Silent reading sessions

c) Writing long essays

d) Grammar exercises only

Answer: a

173. **What enhances reading fluency?**

a) Timed repeated readings

b) Listening only

c) Memorizing passages

d) Ignoring difficult words

Answer: a

174 .**How does task-based learning benefit students?**

a) It replaces all grammar teaching

b) It focuses on meaningful real-world tasks

c) It limits interaction

d) It discourages group work

Answer: b

175. **Which assessment identifies students' learning gaps?**

a) Formative assessment

b) Summative assessment

c) Diagnostic assessment

d) Mid-term exams

Answer: c

176. **Which tool supports auditory learners?**

a) Audiobooks

b) Printed handouts

c) Flashcards

d) Worksheets

Answer: a

177. **What helps improve spelling skills?**

a) Dictation exercises

b) Listening without writing

c) Memorizing only definitions

d) Reading silently

Answer: a

178. **What encourages meaningful language use?**

a) Real-life tasks and scenarios

b) Memorizing grammar rules

c) Avoiding communication

d) Copying sentences

Answer: a

179. **What supports struggling learners?**

a) Providing targeted interventions

b) Assigning more homework

c) Ignoring learning gaps

d) Limiting classroom activities

Answer: a

180. **How does formative assessment benefit students?**

a) By providing continuous feedback for improvement

b) By assigning final grades

c) By ranking students

d) By reducing participation

Answer: a

181. **Which activity enhances both listening and speaking skills?**

a) Group discussions

b) Silent reading

c) Grammar worksheets

d) Multiple-choice quizzes

Answer: a

182. **How does interactive learning benefit students?**

a) It limits participation

b) It engages students actively in the learning process

c) It eliminates individual assessments

d) It replaces classroom activities with self-study

Answer: b

183. **What is the primary focus of diagnostic assessment?**

a) Assigning grades

b) Identifying learning gaps and needs

c) Ranking students in class

d) Reviewing final performance

Answer: b

184. **Which tool best supports vocabulary development?**

a) Grammar books

b) Flashcards and word games

c) Writing essays

d) Silent reading logs

Answer: b

185. **Which activity promotes teamwork and collaboration?**

a) Independent study

b) Group projects and problem-solving activities

c) Individual homework assignments

d) Silent reading sessions

Answer: b

186. **What role does feedback play in language learning?**

a) It discourages student participation

b) It helps students understand areas for improvement

c) It replaces formal assessments

d) It focuses only on errors

Answer: b

187. **Which strategy helps develop oral communication skills?**

a) Role-play and dialogue practice

b) Memorizing textbook content

c) Silent reading

d) Written tests

Answer: a

188. **How does differentiated instruction address student needs?**

a) By providing the same content for all students

b) By tailoring teaching methods to individual learners

c) By focusing only on advanced students

d) By avoiding collaborative activities

Answer: b

189. **What enhances reading comprehension in young learners?**

a) Picture books with simple text

b) Complex academic articles

c) Memorizing definitions

d) Listening without reading

Answer: a

190. **Which teaching strategy encourages student engagement?**

a) Interactive games and activities

b) Long lectures

c) Silent study sessions

d) Memorization exercises

Answer: a

191 .**What supports language retention?**

a) Repeated exposure to words in context

b) Silent reading only

c) Memorizing vocabulary lists without context

d) Avoiding speaking practice

Answer: a

192. **How can teachers promote active participation?**

a) By encouraging group activities and discussions

b) By assigning only independent work

c) By limiting speaking opportunities

d) By focusing solely on written tasks

Answer: a

193. **What is the goal of task-based language teaching?**

a) To complete meaningful real-world tasks

b) To memorize grammar rules

c) To limit speaking activities

d) To focus on written assessments only

Answer: a

194. **Which tool best assesses listening skills?**

a) Audiobook-based quizzes

b) Grammar worksheets

c) Silent reading tasks

d) Spelling tests

Answer: a

195. **How does peer interaction improve learning?**

a) It limits student involvement

b) It encourages collaborative problem-solving

c) It discourages participation

d) It focuses only on individual tasks

Answer: b

196. **Which strategy promotes critical thinking in students?**

a) Engaging in class debates

b) Memorizing textbook answers

c) Skipping difficult topics

d) Relying only on teacher lectures

Answer: a

197. **How does storytelling enhance language learning?**

a) It develops listening and speaking skills

b) It focuses only on grammar rules

c) It reduces the need for vocabulary practice

d) It discourages creative thinking

Answer: a

198. **What is an essential component of formative assessment?**

a) Providing feedback during the learning process

b) Grading students at the end of the course

c) Eliminating class activities

d) Assigning only final exams

Answer: a

199 .**Which activity strengthens vocabulary and usage?**

a) Playing word games and puzzles

b) Listening without speaking

c) Writing without feedback

d) Skimming through texts quickly

Answer: a

200 .**What encourages language practice in a real-life context?**

a) Simulating everyday conversations through role-play

b) Memorizing word lists

c) Avoiding communication outside class

d) Reading silently only

Answer: a

Printed at Repro India Ltd.